The Franklin Delano Roosevelt Memorial

Designed by Lawrence Halprin

Written by David Dillon

Photographed by Alan Ward

S P A C E M A K E R   P R E S S

Washington, DC

Cambridge, MA

Front cover: FDR used "Fireside Chats"
to lift the spirits of the American people.
Sculpture by George Segal.
Art by George Segal is ©George Segal/
Licensed by VAGA, New York, NY
Photograph by Alan Ward

Publisher: James G. Trulove
Photographer: Alan Ward except as noted
Art Director: Sarah Vance
Designer: Elizabeth Reifeiss
Printer: Palace Press International

ISBN: 1-888931-11-6

Dedication

To Connie and Jeff Hall, who lived the memorial's story.

Acknowledgments

Special thanks to archivist Rod Ross of the National Archives
in Washington, DC, for helping to unscramble the files of
the FDR Memorial Commision; to Kathleen Chick, who
provided valuable research assistance; and to Karen Burtis
of the FDR Library, who provided a wide selection of historic
images of FDR.

Contents

4

"... I never forget that I live in a house owned by all the American people and that I have been given their trust. I try always to remember that their deepest problems are human. I constantly talk with those who come to tell me their own points of view— with those who manage the great industries and financial institutions of the country—with those who represent the farmer and the worker—and often, very often with average citizens without high position who come to this house. And constantly I seek to look beyond the doors of the White House, beyond the officialdom of the National Capital, into the hopes and fears of men and women in their homes." —Franklin Delano Roosevelt, "Fireside Chat," April 14, 1938.

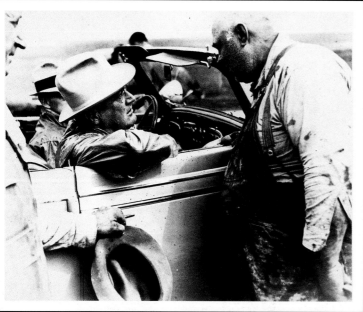

Depression bread line
New York City, 1932 (top)

FDR talking to a homesteader
Jamestown, North Dakota, 1936

FDR at the Casablanca   FDR with Stalin and Churchill at

Fireside Chats:

On unemployment

November 14, 1937.

resident as he spoke
nation last Monday.

FDR and Fala in the

White House study

December 20, 1941.

Two known photographs of
FDR in a wheelchair:
Assembling on the terrace
before a cruise down the
Hudson, Hyde Park, 1937.

The Franklin Delano Roosevelt Memorial meanders 800 feet beside the Potomac Tidal Basin, long and low and, from certain angles, nearly invisible. No columns, friezes, or other classical details adorn its surfaces. The gleaming marble and limestone of official Washington have given way to blocks of pink South Dakota granite, rugged heartland stone, arranged like rooms in an outdoor museum. The rooms are grand and abstract but their contents are precise and personal, spanning the four terms and thirteen years (1933-45) of FDR's presidency.

This was the decisive period in twentieth-century American history, when the nation awoke from its near-fatal slumber to rebuild its shattered economy, defeat fascism, and emerge as an international power. It is a period that, except for military memorials, has gone largely uncelebrated in official Washington. The memorial commemorates Roosevelt's achievements on all these fronts, using fountains, sculpture, and inscriptions to convey the breadth of his vision and the force of his leadership. And it celebrates the courage of those who embraced his message and made his vision real. It is a memorial to national resolve.

At 7.5 acres and $48 million ($42.5 million of it public), the FDR Memorial is also far grander than the one Roosevelt envisioned. "If any memorial is to be erected to me," he confided to Supreme Court Justice Felix Frankfurter in 1941, "I know exactly what I should like it to be. Right in front of the Archives Building [on Pennsylvania Avenue] is a little green triangle. If . . . they are to put up any memorial to me, I should like it to be placed in the center of that green plot. . . . I would like it to consist of a block of stone about the size of this [desk]. I don't care what it is made of, whether limestone or granite or whatnot, but I want it to be plain, without any ornamentation, with the simple carving 'In memory of . . . ' That is all."[1]

This modest request sparked decades of noisy public debate. Some people argued that the president's wishes should be respected and only a modest memorial—a fountain, perhaps, or at most, a rose garden—should be built. Yet to those who had served under Roosevelt, and the

millions more whose lives were changed by his presidency, a block of stone or a few flowerbeds seemed like a rebuke. He was their idol and their inspiration. He had led America out of the Great Depression and through the nightmare of World War II. His social programs provided jobs and hope for millions and altered forever Americans' relationship to their government. Before FDR, the average citizen encountered the federal government mainly when buying stamps at the post office. The country had few banking laws and no security regulations. Its military was barely a step ahead of horse cavalry, while its capital, compared with London or Paris, was a provincial backwater run by avocational politicians on a seasonal basis. Franklin Roosevelt changed the face of modern America, and for doing so, his supporters argued, he deserved a memorial as important as those to Washington, Lincoln, and Jefferson.

For thirty years, FDR's supporters nurtured that dream, defying critics who insisted that the proposed memorial was too expensive, too pompous, and too partisan. Yet even after Congress finally authorized the project in 1978, landscape architect Lawrence Halprin had to wait another twenty years to see it completed. Delays are commonplace for Washington memorials—construction of the Washington Monument took eighty-nine years, the Lincoln Memorial a mere fifty-five—but none surpassed the FDR Memorial for political intrigue and startling reversals. Anything that could go wrong did, from federal budget crises to Roosevelt family protests. At one point or another, everyone involved despaired of its being built.

In dedicating the FDR Memorial on May 2, 1997, President Bill Clinton paid tribute not only to Roosevelt's political genius but to the tenacity of those who preserved his legacy in stone.

"FDR actually wanted no memorial," the president reminded his audience, "[and] for years, none seemed necessary. The America he built was a memorial all around us. From the Golden Gate Bridge to the Grand Coulee Dam; from Social Security to honest financial markets; from an America that has remained the world's indispensable nation to our shared conviction that all Americans must make our journey together. ... But the world turns and memories fade. And now, more than a half-century after he left us, it is right that we go a little beyond his stated wishes and dedicate this memorial as a tribute to Franklin Roosevelt, to Eleanor, and to the remarkable triumphs of their generation."

Ironically, the FDR Memorial opened at a time when cynicism about government and government programs was at a historic high. "Local control" had become the mantra of an entire generation of politicians and civic leaders, who consider Washington the enemy of democracy and personal freedom. Roosevelt, on the other hand, believed unequivocally in government as an agent of social change. When he took office, America was paralyzed by fear and uncertainty, unable to help itself or even to recognize where help might lie. Only a strong and compassionate federal government, he insisted, could make the nation whole again. So he created the Works Progress Administration and the Civilian Conservation Corps, the monumental Tennessee Valley Authority and the scholarly Index of American Design. No corner of America remained untouched by his New Deal programs. To critics, including most of the old-time political bosses, these programs amounted to a usurpation of the democratic will, while to Roosevelt they represented the fulfillment of a fundamental social contract. As he noted in his second inaugural address, "The test of our progress is not whether we add more to the abundance of those who have much; it is whether we provide enough for those who have too little."

For those who share Roosevelt's political philosophy, the FDR Memorial is a deserved and long overdue recognition of singular leadership and courage. But even those who find his philosophy of government abhorrent may still agree with Lawrence Halprin's description of the memorial as "a tribute not only to one man, but to the people of the United States who went through this. It is a memorial to democracy."[2]

The original FDR Memorial in front of the
National Archives on Pennsylvania Avenue,
Washington, DC.

Franklin Delano Roosevelt's death in 1945 produced a national catharsis of grief. Schools were closed. Crowds wept uncontrollably as his cortege passed and for years afterward families kept his picture on their kitchen walls. Across America swept an ominous feeling that FDR had died at the wrong time, while the nation was still at risk.

In July 1946, fifteen months after FDR's death, a congressional resolution was introduced creating the Franklin Delano Roosevelt Memorial Commission "for the purpose of formulating plans for the design, construction and location of a permanent memorial to FDR in the city of Washington, District of Columbia, or its immediate environs."

The sponsors wanted to act quickly, while memories of FDR's accomplishments were still fresh. But in a preview of things to come, the Commission wasn't actually established until August 1955, nine years later. In the interim, experts debated the likely cost of the project, even though no design existed. Some questioned the appropriateness of memorializing a president so soon after his death. Twenty-five or fifty years seemed a more decent interval, after history had its say.

"If the Lincoln Memorial had been erected in 1866, it might have mentioned the battle of Gettysburg and ignored the Address," a skeptical columnist wrote in the *New Republic*. "By the same token a memorial to Roosevelt erected now may mention the wrong things."[3] And why Roosevelt, others wanted to know, when so many equally deserving Americans—Calvin Coolidge, for example—had no memorials?

The Commission pushed ahead anyway, led by FDR's attorney general Francis Biddle. In June 1958, it selected a 27-acre site in West Potomac Park, between the river and the Tidal Basin. The same site had been recommended by the 1901 McMillan Plan (which refined and amplified Pierre L'Enfant's 1791 plan for Washington) for a fourth presidential memorial, affording it an impeccable political pedigree.

"The memorial will not be merely another 'monument,'" promised Chairman Biddle, "but will be designed to beautify a great stretch of unimproved land along the water and tie it in with the three other great memorials—with Washington, Jefferson, and Lincoln—where Roosevelt belongs."[4]

Using a $150,000 congressional appropriation, the Commission organized a national design competition with Edmund Bacon, executive director of the Philadelphia Planning Commission, as advisor, and Portland, Oregon, architect Pietro Belluschi as head of the jury.[5] The competition, held in two stages, was open to all registered architects who were residents of the United States—a controversial provision since it excluded Alvar Aalto, Le Corbusier, and other renowned European architects—as well as to teams of landscape architects, sculptors, and painters provided one was a registered architect.

The Commission was silent on the form of the memorial, saying only that designers should "look to the character and work of Franklin Roosevelt to [provide] the theme of a memorial that will do him the honor he deserves and transmit his living image to future generations."

The first stage attracted 574 submissions, ranging from primitive stelae and classical pavilions to monumental bronze statues and meticulously sculpted landscapes. The prevailing style was monumental and brutalist, consisting of exposed concrete beams and columns joined in dramatic and often intimidating ways. It was architecture of bold gestures rather than subtle refinements, and focused more on the details of its own construction than on the needs of its users. The submissions were thinned to six for the second round, including an elliptical earthen bowl with a fountain by landscape architects Sasaki, Walker & Associates; four cantilevered planes sheltering four rectangular courtyards by the Abraham W. Geller Group; and a circular granite mound with a hovering roof and a statue of Roosevelt by architect and sculptor Rolf Myller. Pittsburgh architect Tasso Katselas proposed an open pavilion also with a monumental bust of the president, while architects Joseph Wehrer and Harold Borkin of the University of Michigan presented a series of sloping

22

The 27-acre memorial site, showing Rolf Myller's design in relationship to the Washington, Lincoln and Jefferson Memorials.

1960 competition finalists:
First place William Pedersen and
Bradford Tilney, architects; Norman
Hoberman, sculptor (top).

Abraham W. Geller Group,
architects; Richard Haag,
landscape architect.

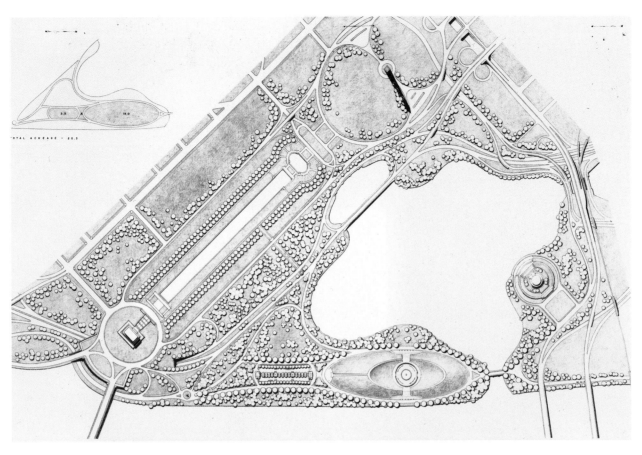

Sasaki, Walker & Associates,
landscape architects and planners;
Luders & Associates, architects (top).

Joseph Wehrer and Harold Borkin,
architects; William Johnson,
landscape architect.

Proposal by Tasso Katselas, architect (top).

Proposal by Rolf Myller, architect and sculptor (below).

granite walls surrounding a large central court to be used for ceremonies related to FDR's life and work.

On December 30, 1960, the jury selected a design by William Pedersen and Bradford Tilney of New York City, with Norman Hoberman as sculptor. It consisted of eight soaring concrete and marble tablets, the tallest rising 165 feet, inscribed with quotations from Roosevelt's speeches and arranged to allow views of the Potomac and the Tidal Basin. Rather than deeds, the design made Roosevelt's words his monument.

Chairman Biddle praised the winning design for its "tremendous sense of power,"[6] while prominent architects lauded its appropriateness to its time. William Lescaze, codesigner of the landmark Philadelphia Savings Fund Society Building, called it "a simple, strong, sculptural and architectural statement in terms of today." Philip Johnson commended the "powerful, almost primitive tablets that form a splendid expression of 20th-century art." The FDR Memorial Commission approved the design in 1962.[7]

But the splendor was lost on the press and the public, who labeled the design "instant Stonehenge" and a "set of bookends just out of the deep freeze." Even jury chairman Belluschi sounded underwhelmed. "I hate to bring up Moses and his tablets," he said, "but this is a sort of version of them."[8]

The debate soon devolved into a referendum on Modernism, with the young Turks and the old guard squaring off over questions of style and intention. What was a Modern memorial? Was such a thing even possible in a godless, antiheroic age? Some defended the Pedersen and Tilney design on the grounds that not to do so would sabotage the Modern movement, while others attacked it for its hostility to accepted classical precedents. "Modernists have failed once again," chided one critic. "It is a pity that [the jury's] bias should cloud the fact that there are Americans willing and able to work in the style (i.e. classical) which, after all, belongs in the nation's capital."[9] One fourth of the submissions were classical, but as the debate ground on month after month in the newspapers and professional magazines, fact took a back seat to attitude.

Stunned by the uproar, the Commission asked Pedersen and Tilney to revise their design. The second version was 35 feet lower than the first so as not to compete with neighboring memorials, and included a large statue of President Roosevelt at the center. It was promptly approved by the FDR Memorial Commission and, just as quickly, rejected by the powerful Commission of Fine Arts, the presidentially appointed guardians of public works in Washington, which concluded that it "lacked repose."

For the next two years, the Pedersen and Tilney design ricocheted back and forth among review boards and congressional committees, each searching vainly for some patch of common ground. In 1964, the FDR Memorial Commission and the Commission of Fine Arts both approved Tilney and Pedersen's second revised design, only to have Congressman James Roosevelt, FDR's oldest son, denounce it on the floor of the House. "We don't like it, and I'm sure Father wouldn't either," he reported confidently.

Opposition from the Roosevelt family killed fund-raising and any hope of a congressional endorsement. In April 1965, Pedersen and Tilney resigned the commission.

Unwilling to risk a second open competition, the Commission solicited proposals from fifty-five leading American architects, including I. M. Pei, Paul Rudolph, and Philip Johnson. In January 1966, after reviewing the responses, the Commission selected Marcel Breuer, designer of the UNESCO Headquarters in Paris, the Whitney Museum of American Art, and other Modernist icons. Only Mies van der Rohe had a loftier reputation among progressive architects, and none was more beloved than this self-effacing Hungarian émigré.

Although Breuer had passed up the first competition, he said he admired what Pedersen and Tilney had done—and proceeded to do

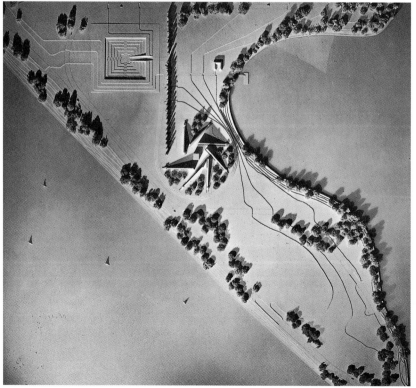

Elevation, plan, and perspective
of 1966 design by Marcel Breuer.

something similar: a ring of seven rough granite darts, approximately 60 feet high, pinwheeling around a 32-foot cube of polished granite inscribed with a photographic portrait of FDR. Narrow pools of water ran beside each dart, making them appear to float, but instead of inscriptions, Breuer proposed recorded excerpts from FDR's speeches. "It is pure geometry," Breuer said, noting that his walls slanted toward the earth the way Roosevelt's words reached out to the American people.

The critics were unimpressed, tearing into Breuer's design as enthusiastically as they had Pedersen and Tilney's. "Disrespectful and frivolous," snapped one member of the Commission of Fine Arts. "This might have been all right for the Cabinet of Dr. Caligari," chided another, "but it doesn't have much to do with today." Several members singled out the recorded speeches as an idea worthy of Forest Lawn Cemetery. [10]

The Commission of Fine Arts unanimously rejected the design in January 1967. For the next two years, sympathetic senators on the FDR Memorial Commission, led by Eugene McCarthy of Minnesota, tried to circumvent Fine Arts and win congressional approval of the Breuer design. Their resolutions never made it out of committee, and Breuer finally quit in frustration in 1969.

Another five years passed, during which time various proposals for living memorials to FDR—parks, rose gardens, waterways—surfaced and sank. One group even suggested planting windbreaks on the Great Plains in honor of FDR's soil conservation programs. These discarded solutions further underscored the problem of try-ing to memorialize a president not yet safely dead. Instead of a commemoration, the memorial was becoming a tool for settling old political scores.

Embarrassed and increasingly desperate, the Memorial Commission turned to the Department of the Interior for help in planning and designing the memorial. The department advertised the project in government publications, received ninety replies, and selected seven architects for interviews. In May 1974, the Commission chose San Francisco landscape architect Lawrence Halprin. It already knew Halprin's work through the efforts of one of its members, Oregon Senator Mark Hatfield, who admired the architect's Lovejoy Plaza and Auditorium Forecourt fountains in Portland and lobbied the other commissioners vigorously on Halprin's behalf. [11]

Unlike previous designs, Halprin's contained no single dominant object. It was instead a low landscape of stone walls, waterfalls, and dense clusters of trees and flowering shrubs. It was horizontal rather than vertical, open instead of closed, a memorial that told a story and encouraged participation rather than mute admiration.

Halprin's conceptual design was approved unanimously by the FDR Memorial Commission in May 1975 and by the Commission of Fine Arts in June 1976. The final design was approved in March 1978. Congress authorized construction—though no money—in July 1981. Nevertheless, it appeared that after three decades of turmoil, the Franklin Delano Roosevelt Memorial was on its way at last. As it turned out, the approvals were only the prologue to an even more painful series of delays.

Halprin's model of the FDR Memorial

as approved by Congress in 1978.

The tenacity of FDR's supporters was matched by that of Lawrence Halprin, who after winning the 1974 competition, found himself on a political roller coaster for twenty-three years, as budget crises, political wrangling, and bureaucratic inertia repeatedly stalled the project. It was a commission for a street fighter as well as a landscape architect, and Halprin proved to be both.

Born in 1916 in the Bronx, where his father was president of a scientific instruments firm, Halprin studied horticulture at Cornell University and the University of Wisconsin. In 1941 he migrated to Harvard to join Breuer, Walter Gropius, and, most importantly, Christopher Tunnard, whose seminal book, *Gardens in the Modern Landscape*, presented landscape architecture as a great synthesizing discipline instead of merely a footnote to the architecture curriculum. The study of gardens, Tunnard argued, was an introduction to the study of parks, wilderness, and cities. Landscape architecture had important social and civic dimensions as well as esthetic ones. Such views, entirely consistent with Gropius's Bauhaus principles, found a receptive audience in the young Halprin, who quickly became a Tunnard disciple and later a close friend.

"The thing that resonated with me was that Tunnard didn't draw a line between design and social issues," Halprin recalls. "Good housing and good landscape were all part of the same thing. I've never forgotten that."

After serving as a lieutenant in the U.S. Navy during World War II, Halprin worked four years for landscape architect Thomas Church, the guru of contemporary California garden design. Church encouraged him to experiment with plants and color, and to think of gardens not simply as private spaces but as settings for human activity. Halprin would subsequently apply that insight to the design of everything from public parks and plazas to his own backyard, which he transformed into a stage and studio for his wife, the dancer and choreographer Anna Schumann. Church also sent him into the field to learn construction and how to integrate architecture with landscape.

"Tommy was a brilliant site planner who could conceptualize on a big scale," Halprin said. "But he was the opposite of Tunnard. He had no social views at all. He was just a good professional."

Halprin left Church's office in 1949 to form Lawrence Halprin and Associates, where he has practiced ever since. By the time he was selected for the FDR Memorial, he had completed a string of impressive projects: Lovejoy Plaza and the Auditorium Forecourt fountain in Portland, Oregon; Seattle's Freeway Park; the Sea Ranch condominiums on the northern California coast; America's first transit mall in Minneapolis; and San Francisco's Ghirardelli Square, the prototype for the ubiquitous festival markets of the 1970s and 1980s.

In different ways, these projects all illustrate the central themes of Halprin's career: the attraction of natural forms, especially wild and primitive ones; the magic of water; and the importance of group interaction, what he calls "collective creativity," as both a generator and an energizer of design. Good spaces, for Halprin, are defined by human activity, not geometry. "They require total involvement and are never purely visual," is how he describes them.

Halprin's office in San Francisco became a center for participatory design, epitomized by his "Taking-Part Workshops," in which the members (architects, clients, users) respond to a series of scripted questions by writing, sketching, or performing. The responses are then "scored," as in a piece of music, to create a starting point and ideally a story line for a design. These workshops, part charrette and part encounter group, may last a few hours or be spread over several days or weeks, and involve a handful of people or several hundred. The basic design for the FDR Memorial grew out of workshops in Halprin's office, which were later expanded to include artists, commissioners, and public officials.

Lovejoy Fountain, Portland, Oregon.

Halprin's selection was hailed a victory for naturalness and human scale over chilly monumentality, even though his design covered nearly 8 acres and rested on a massive concrete platform sunk into an island that was created in the 1890s by the Army Corps of Engineers. His idea of "natural" was not the Romantic notion of a pristine landscape but the Modern one of man and nature intertwined and inseparable. And yet compared to preceding designs, Halprin's seemed natural. Instead of spiraling fins and soaring concrete tablets, he arranged low granite walls into outdoor rooms, then filled them with water, plants, and art to create a concentrated and abstracted natural landscape.

"I made it a narrative," Halprin explained, "and wanted people to learn about Roosevelt through all the senses, not just sight."

Even though Halprin's design was softer and more inviting than its predecessors, it did not silence congressional critics. At $50 million, it would be the costliest memorial ever built. How could they justify such a public expense, legislators asked, when Roosevelt himself had requested a "plain" block of stone, "without any ornamentation"? Periodically the critics turned on the FDR Memorial Commission itself, pointing out that it had spent $500,000 of taxpayer money with nothing to show for it. "One of our hoariest boondoggles," fumed syndicated columnist Jack Anderson in urging its dissolution.[12] Spread over twenty-five years, the half million was barely enough to pay for stamps and the salary of one overworked secretary. But it made great headlines.

Congress's parsimony had many sources, from concern about the ripple effects of the 1974 Arab oil embargo and California's Proposition 13, which limited property tax increases to 2 percent per year, to lingering resentment of FDR's social policies and programs. "There are still some people who are against any memorial to the president," charged Memorial Commission Chairman Eugene Keogh. More to the point, Roosevelt's core constituency was dying off; the power of key supporters, such as organized labor, was waning.

"There was a lot of second-guessing of Roosevelt going on," adds Halprin. "For a long time after his death, his reputation wasn't very high. Then, like Churchill's, it began to rebound."

The low point came in 1979, when the Department of the Interior suddenly abandoned the project it had previously championed. "Fifty million is an unreasonably high figure for any memorial," Secretary Cecil Andrus explained, while hinting that he might be receptive to something more modest. Trees, for example. FDR loved trees, Andrus reminded his critics. Even listed his occupation as "tree grower."

"Everyone thought that was the kiss of death," Halprin said, "but we found ways to do a little bit of work each year, waiting for things to change."

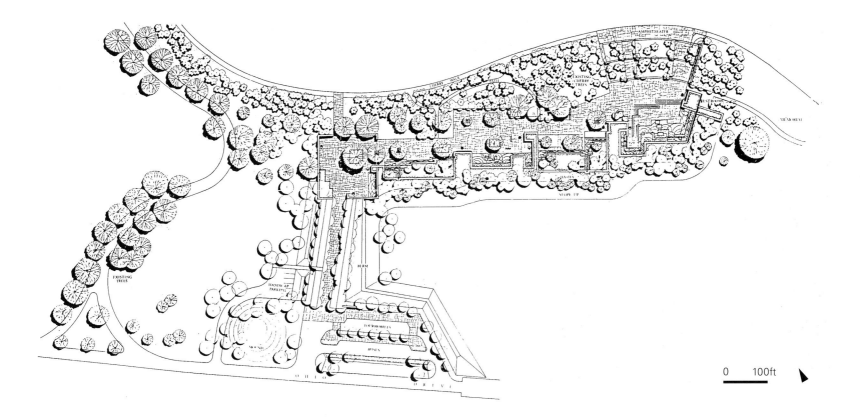

0   100ft

Halprin had already chosen three sculptors for the memorial (George Segal, Leonard Baskin, and Robert Graham) and produced a persuasive film for Congress and the various commissions. Now he set about editing the original design, eliminating 500 feet of granite wall, an elaborate interpretative center, and several fountains. These changes reduced the cost to approximately $24 million, half the original estimate, but still not low enough to win over critics in Congress.

The stalemate continued until 1989, when Congressman Claude Pepper—an ardent New Dealer, champion of "Gray Rights" for the elderly, and then-chairman of the FDR Memorial Commission—made an impassioned plea to his colleagues for support. Eighty-eight and dying of cancer, he left his bed at Walter Reed Army hospital to remind them that Roosevelt was a great man and a great president who had changed the tenor of American life. He deserved a great memorial. Reportedly, there wasn't a dry eye in the house when he finished. A few days later President Bush called on him at the hospital and, from his bed, Pepper made another appeal for funding. This time the money came through. After a few last-minute procedural delays, groundbreaking took place in 1991 and construction finally began in 1994.

Weathered and sometimes cranky as a winter bear, Lawrence Halprin becomes almost wistful in talking about the FDR Memorial.

"I was a Socialist, so all of this has tremendous meaning for me in my gut," he said just prior to the dedication. "It's the story of my life. It's the story of my college roommate's life and of most of my friends' lives. It's the story of liberalism at the end of the war, and of deep, genuine optimism about the world and the future. I don't know that we'll ever recapture that feeling again."

The FDR Memorial is a shrewdly choreographed sequence of spaces and moods that attempts to balance the demands of biography and history. Initially spare and silent, it grows louder and more intense during the Great Depression and World War II, reaching an emotional crescendo with Roosevelt's death in 1945, then receding into cautious optimism as America enters the postwar era.

The memorial consists of four large rooms, connected by landscaped corridors, that recall Roosevelt's four terms, the Four Freedoms, and the four continental time zones. Yet unlike the overblown compositions of Pedersen and Tilney or Marcel Breuer, Halprin's design cannot be understood at a glance. The large rooms are composed of numerous small events involving sculpture, fountains, and plantings. Spaces turn out to be more fragmentary than they appear, and views more partial, so that visitors must investigate for themselves what's just around the corner or behind the wall.

The fluidity of Halprin's design owes something to modern dance and, more specifically, to the influence of his wife, Anna Schumann. They studied together at Harvard and absorbed the same Bauhaus philosophy concerning the fundamental unity of all the arts. They subsequently collaborated on pieces for Schumann's breakthrough Dancers Workshop, which took dance out of the theater and onto the streets of San Francisco and other cities. Her pieces were usually improvisational and inspired by nature or significant social and political events, such as the Watts Riots of the 1960s. Halprin designed

sets and costumes for many of these pieces, and still occasionally refers to himself as a choreographer and set designer.

"I felt early on that an understanding of movement was what was needed to understand what landscape architecture was all about," he said.

In the FDR Memorial, Halprin identifies entrances and exits while allowing visitors to choose specific paths. They can start at the main plaza and walk through to the Jefferson Memorial, or begin at the Jefferson, clearly the secondary entrance, and make the trip in reverse. The first offers a tightly structured sequence of rooms and corridors, each linked visually and chronologically to the next, while the second provides a looser, more leisurely arrangement of spaces coupled with more sweeping views of the Tidal Basin and monumental Washington.

Approaching from the west, the Lincoln Memorial in the background, visitors cross a granite plaza flanked by a gift shop and double rows of zelkova trees to a stark granite wall inscribed with the words:

Franklin Delano Roosevelt
President of the United States
1933-1945

The inscription is a kind of minimalist marquee that announces the title of the show without a hint of what's inside. Immediately to its right is a narrow slot—Halprin calls it his "medieval gate"—leading to an alcove containing a bronze relief of the presidential seal by Tom Hardy. The alcove is purposely spare and silent, the calm before the gathering storm.

The alcove leads to the first large room, devoted to Roosevelt's first term. Despite the bleakness of events, the mood is generally upbeat, as epitomized by Robert Graham's bas relief *First Inaugural*. And immediately to the east is a dramatic postcard view of the Washington Monument, with the Tidal Basin as the foreground. In his 1974 design, Halprin

36

had placed the main entrance on the south or Potomac side of the memorial, on axis with the Washington Monument. The National Park Service objected to losing its playing fields, and Halprin himself eventually concluded that the grand axial view was too much of an introduction. What could he do for an encore? He relocated the main entrance to the west and made the dramatic monument view a surprise, as though someone had pulled back the drapes from a gigantic picture window.

At the center of Room II stand three groups of bronze sculptures by George Segal, each revealing a face of the Great Depression through an unusual mixture of literalness and ghostly imprecision. In one, a despairing Appalachian couple appear before their crumbling farm house, like figures in a WPA photograph by Dorothea Lange or Walker Evans. To their right five men in overcoats and crushed hats wait in a bread line, epitomizing the indignity of want. Across the room, a solitary figure sits next to a radio listening to one of Roosevelt's "fireside chats." Despite his patrician background, Roosevelt spoke the language of the common man. Instead of speeches and addresses, he gave seemingly impromptu chats in which he used homely analogies to drive home complex political points. He was the first real media president.

Segal, Graham, and Leonard Baskin were all chosen from a list put together by Halprin and an advisory committee. (Neil Estern was added at the insistence of Memorial Commission Chairman Eugene Keogh, in whose congressional district Estern lived, while Tom Hardy was brought on later.) As with the architects in the original competition, only American artists were eligible. Once chosen, the artists were required to participate in a series of intense workshops, called "jam sessions," in which they and Halprin worked out the relationships between the sculpture and the rest of the memorial.[13]

As described in the Memorial Commission's 1978 *Report to the President and Congress*, "the sculptors, the calligrapher and the designer of the memorial explored at length and in depth, over a

Lawrence Halprin on a 1984 site visit to oversee construction of the memorial.

period of days, their views of Franklin Delano Roosevelt, the nature of public art, the significant relationship of their own work to each other's, and the major themes to be depicted and by whom. They spoke together, ate together, made drawings, argued, and slowly began to form a collective preliminary sculptural view of an iconographic response to the issue of Roosevelt's presidency within the spatial context of the memorial as designed."

From all accounts, these were tense and draining sessions in which the artists had to overcome their fear of collaboration and their over-developed sense of territoriality. "I never had so much help being creative," Segal quipped after one of them.

Two critical components were an 80-foot model of the memorial prepared by Halprin's office, and an image bank, also from Halprin, containing familiar photos, newsreels, and cartoons of the president. The first gave the sculptors a necessary sense of scale, while the second provided inspiration for their work, which Halprin insisted be bronze, figurative, and intimately related to both the walls and the inscriptions. No free-standing pieces, and nothing abstract. "Abstract sculpture didn't mean anything to me at all in this context," he said.

Roosevelt's response to the Great Depression was "a New Deal for the American people," expressed through the dozens of social programs depicted in Robert Graham's piece of the same name. The work consists of large bas reliefs of tools, projects, and workers, and five freestanding columns on which the wall images reappear as negative impressions. Within a few weeks of the memorial's opening, sections of the reliefs and the columns had been burnished by thousands of trailing fingers.

The most dramatic feature of the FDR Memorial, as in most of Halprin's best work, is water. It is simultaneously focal point, background, and metaphor. "Water in my work is never an abstraction," he says. "It is not glass. I use it as something that has emotional and experiential weight."

The thundering waterfalls of Room II, for example, dramatize the scope of the Tennessee Valley Authority, which harnessed raging flood waters and turned them into electricity for millions of rural families. Elsewhere, Halprin uses pools, fountains, dams, waterwalls, and veils to create moods, underscore ideas, and drown out the roar of the jets from nearby National Airport.

Water provides a narrative thread in FDR's life as well. He sailed the waters of Campobello as a young man, began his political career as Assistant Secretary of the Navy under Woodrow Wilson, and, after being stricken with polio in 1921, spent nearly seven years in therapy at Warm Springs, Georgia. "The water put me where I am, and the water has to put me back," Roosevelt said.

As World War II approaches, the waters of the memorial grow more turbulent and threatening, bursting through walls and drowning out reflection. Likewise, the pink granite walls, rough but regular till now, gradually become jagged and unstable, until in Room III they literally split and topple onto the plaza, as though struck by a bomb. The combination of roaring water and solemn inscriptions ("We must be the great arsenal of democracy") underscore the menace of the moment. The FDR of this room, and these years, is the statesman and commander in chief, epitomized by Neil Estern's monumental bronze showing him wearing his signature cape and seated in a high-backed chair. With his massive head and purposeful stare, he is magisterial, Lincolnesque.

Given the tortuous history of the memorial, it was perhaps inevitable that even this conventional sculpture would arouse controversy. After Roosevelt contracted polio, he never again walked unaided. Yet he went to extraordinary lengths to conceal his disability from the public, including colluding with press photographers never to show him in braces or a wheelchair. Only two such images have been discovered, both in the Roosevelt home at Hyde Park. Most depict him as smiling and robust, prepared for anything.

Many people, Halprin among them, believed that Roosevelt should be portrayed as he portrayed himself.

"Everybody in my generation was vaguely aware that he was crippled," Halprin recalled. "But we also saw him every week in newsreels, going everywhere, doing everything. We didn't really think that much about it. If that was how he wanted to be seen, fine."

Advocates for the disabled objected that not showing Roosevelt in a wheelchair was an insult to his memory. His disability gave him his character, they argued, and created a special bond with the American people. A 1996 Gallup poll showed that 73 percent of them favored a memorial that recognized FDR's disability. So in July 1997, President Clinton signed a law calling for "an addition of a permanent statue, bas relief, or other similar structure" to recognize that President Roosevelt led the nation through its darkest hours while in a wheelchair.

To some observers, this seemed like a reprise of the Vietnam Memorial controversy of the 1980s, when veterans' groups pressured Congress into creating what amounted to a second memorial of bronze infantrymen near the entrance to Maya Lin's abstract design. In that case, adding the sculptures was a condition for constructing the memorial, whereas additions to the FDR Memorial are considered "enhancements" of the existing narrative. Halprin is currently working with an advisory committee to come up with an appropriate addition.

Room III concludes with a spare, silent niche commemorating Roosevelt's death. No rushing water or lush plants, only Leonard Baskin's 30-foot bas relief of Roosevelt's funeral cortege stretching above a reflecting pool, a somber counterpart to Robert Graham's upbeat First Inaugural in Room I. Reliefs are traditional on the tombs of heroes, and this one asks us to meditate on loss in both national and personal terms.

"We lost Roosevelt at the wrong time," Halprin said, echoing the theme of Baskin's relief. "Things got away from us that he had under control. We would have done better if he'd lived a bit longer."

Eleanor Roosevelt, dressed in overcoat and sensible shoes but without her politically incorrect fur wrap, marks the transition between Rooms III and IV, the world of war and the ambiguous, untested world of international negotiation and compromise that FDR made possible. First Lady, presidential confidante, crusader for women's rights and racial justice, she occupies her own niche in the memorial as she did in life.

Room IV might be subtitled "FDR's Legacy." The war has ended; the Four Freedoms are intact; a new era of international cooperation has begun with the Marshall Plan and the United Nations, to which Eleanor Roosevelt was a delegate. Unlike Room III, this section is animated and expansive. Water gushes from rocks in strong festive bursts. Space is no longer confined by walls and corridors, but spills out into a broad amphitheater where the public can gather for concerts and celebrations. Its spirit is summarized in Roosevelt's valedictory quotation: "The only limit to our realization of tomorrow will be our doubts of today. Let us move forward with strong and active faith." The quotation echoes the famous statement from FDR's first inaugural address, "The only thing we have to fear is fear itself," and provides a fitting coda to the story of his presidency.

The Franklin Delano Roosevelt Memorial does what memorials have traditionally done—recalls great persons and events and invites us to reflect on them. It also celebrates a generation and an era, which most memorials do not. Yet because of its size and prominence, the FDR Memorial merits close critical scrutiny.

Lawrence Halprin has described the memorial as a series of serendipitous events occurring between two fixed points. We don't gaze at it in silent awe, as we do at Daniel Chester French's monumental statue of Abraham Lincoln. The FDR Memorial is a participatory work in which our understanding of Roosevelt and his times grows as we walk from room to room, reflecting upon each inscription and each piece of sculpture. In this respect, it anticipates the more austere and abstract Vietnam Veterans Memorial on the Mall, which must also be entered in order to be understood. What might Maya Lin have created had the FDR Memorial been built in the 1970s instead of the 1990s?

If the FDR Memorial is as much park as monument, it is also a park in which some paths are more appealing than others. The primary sequence, from the entry plaza to the Jefferson Memorial, combines clarity and mystery. We know where to go, but not what we will find once we get there. At almost every step we are confronted with choices and surprises, which Halprin heightens by skillfully mixing large spaces and small, hard edges and soft, light and shadow. Though tightly choreographed, the memorial feels open, fluid, and kinetic.

But few stories read as well backward as forward. If the straightforward, chronological route is integrated and dramatic, the approach from the Jefferson Memorial seems diffuse and static. The entire memorial stands off to one side, devoid of anticipation and linear progression. The views become panoramic and the divisions between rooms blurred, to the point that visitors can be halfway through a room before they recognize it. The Tidal Basin

side is particularly weak. Instead of an edge there is only a loose gathering of trees and shrubs trailing off toward the water. Lacking the crisp definition of the rest of the memorial, this area seems like an afterthought.

Halprin's subject from start to finish is Roosevelt the politician, statesman, and commander in chief, the public personality rather than the private man. The memorial captures Roosevelt's dignity and heroic resolve, but not the wit and jauntiness that made him such an appealing leader to millions of Americans. The cocktail shaker and the cigarette holder have vanished. The inscriptions are Horatian, the tone mostly didactic and declamatory. Instead of allowing visitors to make up their own minds about FDR, Halprin spells things out, sometimes with exclamation points. The toppled boulders in Room III, for example, are inscribed with the statement "I Hate War," as though rubble couldn't speak for itself. Such overstatement makes the FDR Memorial dramatically different from the Vietnam Veteran's Memorial, which makes no explicit statement about the war and allows no intervention between visitors and the individual names on the wall.

This didactic tone is reinforced by the sculpture, mostly narrative pieces by artists with similar views of Roosevelt and the New Deal. The work is all technically accomplished and, thanks to Halprin's program, superbly integrated with the rest of the memorial. But none of it challenges conventional impressions of Roosevelt or enlarges the boundaries of public art. Robert Graham's *First Inaugural* was derived from a newsreel, while Leonard Baskin's bas relief of the funeral cortege and Neil Estern's statue of Roosevelt came straight from Halprin's image bank. While the images are familiar, and therefore immediately engaging, they are also iconic and ultimately too easy. Only Robert Graham's relief, *Social Programs*, makes us pause, probe, and question.

As the first major memorial in Washington by a landscape architect, the FDR Memorial has unquestionable historic value,

40

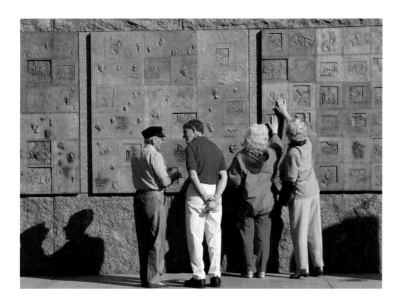

although Halprin's planting plan is very conservative. He preserved many existing elms and Japanese cherry trees and sprinkled pines atop the granite walls to create a canopy. He also added azaleas, rhododendrons, and dogwoods for a burst of spring color. The plantings provide shade and softness and connect the memorial to its immediate surroundings. But the precedents that drive the design are more remote: Lovejoy Plaza in Portland, Seattle's Freeway Park, and portions of Levi Strauss Plaza in San Francisco. The FDR Memorial contains the same rugged cliffs and thundering waterfalls, the same layout of roofless rectangular rooms, and the same celebration of gateway, node, and corridor. It is both a reprise of Halprin's career and a bridge between the heroic classicism of the first half of the century, when mass and verticality were all, and the abstract minimalism of the Vietnam Veterans Memorial, in which mass reclines and memorial merges with landscape.

The unarguable triumph of the FDR Memorial is its accessibility, not simply to the disabled but to everyone. It has attracted ten thousand visitors a day since it opened and possesses remarkable cross-generational appeal. Grandparents use it to tell their grandchildren about the Depression and World War II. The grandchildren in turn clamber into FDR's lap or pose with the larger-than-life-size model of his dog Fala. People rub the sculptures and have their pictures taken with the men in the bread line. A few weeks after the memorial opened, the National Park Service declared the pools and fountains off limits because too many children were using them as a beach and playground. Foot dangling is still permitted, however. Such popular enthusiasm is a tribute not only to Lawrence Halprin's understanding of Roosevelt but to his talent, visible in all his major work, for transforming viewers into participants.

41

"We intend that the design for the Franklin Delano Roosevelt Memorial be a more complete experience and, instead of one isolated symbol, that it emphasize the special qualities which only experience over time can create. Our intention is to make a memorial whose environmental qualities are primarily experiential rather than purely visual—one which is evocative, involving and appropriate for all ages and all people."—Lawrence Halprin, May 1975.

Tom Hardy's "Presidential Seal" in Room I announces the theme of everything that follows.

Next page: West Potomac Park offers a dramatic natural setting for the memorial.

Hundreds of flowering shrubs, such as
these azaleas in the forecourt, provide
seasonal color throughout the memorial.

Pink granite walls and paving form a
series of spare modern spaces that tell
the story of FDR's presidency.

FIRST TERM

Previous page: In panorama, the memorial unfolds like chapters in a historical novel.

The personal anguish of the Great Depression is depicted in three bronze sculptures by George Segal: "Rural Couple," "The Bread Line," and "Fireside Chat".

I NEV... ...ORGET THAT
I L... ...N A HOUSE
OWN... ...Y ALL THE
AM... ...AN PEOPLE
AND ... ...I HAVE BEEN
GIV... ...HEIR TRUST.

*The social programs of the New Deal,
presented in Robert Graham's two-part
bas relief, gave jobs and hope to
millions.*

*Next page: Room II unites the
misery of the bread line with the hope
generated by public works projects
such as Tennessee Valley Authority.*

IT IS TIME TO EXTEND PLANNING TO A WIDER FIELD, IN THIS INSTANCE COMPREHENDING IN ONE GREAT PROJECT MANY STATES DIRECTLY CONCERNED WITH THE BASIN OF ONE OF OUR GREATEST RIVERS.   TENNESSEE VALLEY AUTHORITY

The many moods of water in the FDR Memorial are reflected in the rush of a waterfall and the calm of an adjacent reflecting pool.

GREATEST RIVERS
CONCERNED WITH THE BU
IN ONE GREAT PROJECT WA
HELD, IN THIS INSTANCE CO
IT IS TIME TO EXTEND PLANNI

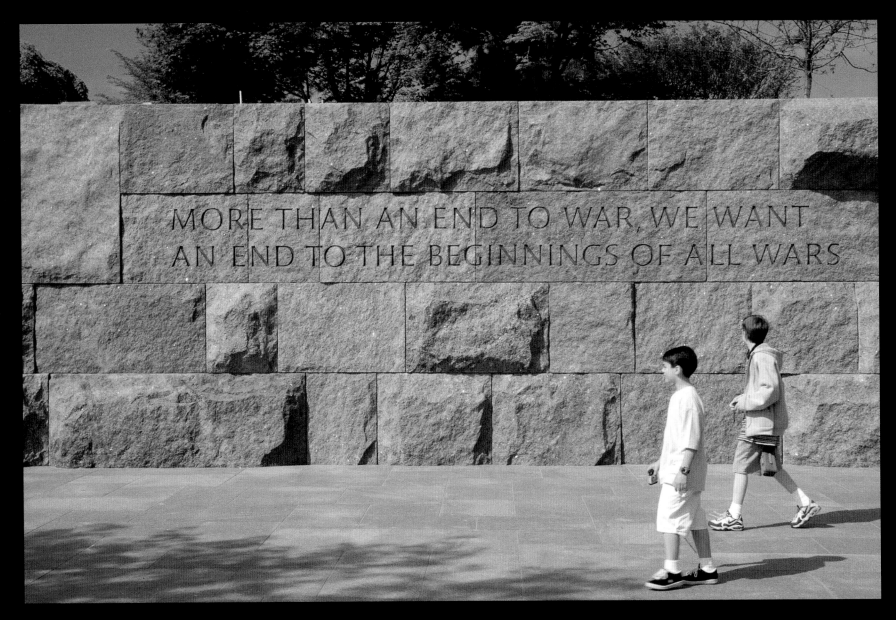

Previous page: The granite rubble in
Room III suggests the physical
destruction of the war.

The quotation is from an undelivered
Jefferson Day speech scheduled for
April 13, 1945, the day after the
president's death.

Eleanor Roosevelt, independent
and courageous as First Lady, was
America's first delegate to the
United Nations.

The somber, statesman-like Roosevelt
of Neil Estern's monumental bronze
surveys the memorial and his own
presidency.

Next page: The memorial's final room
is dedicated to peace and provides a
festive coda to two decades of
deprivation and destruction.

74

Final plan as built in 1997

1 First term 1933-1936

2 Second Term1937-1940

3 Third Term 1941-1944

4 Fourth Term 1945

A Information
Bookshop

B *The Presidential Seal*
Tom Hardy

C Inaugural Fountain

D *The First Inaugural*
Robert Graham

E Pool of Trust

F *Fireside Chat*
George Segal

G *Bread Lines*
George Segal

H *Rural Couple*
George Segal

I *Social Programs*
Robert Graham

J TVA Cascade

K Civil Liberty Pool

L War Room Fountain

M *FDR with Fala*
Neil Estern

N *The Funeral Cortege*
Leonard Baskin

O Funeral Cortege Pool

P *Eleanor Roosevelt*
Neil Estern

Q Four Freedoms Fountain

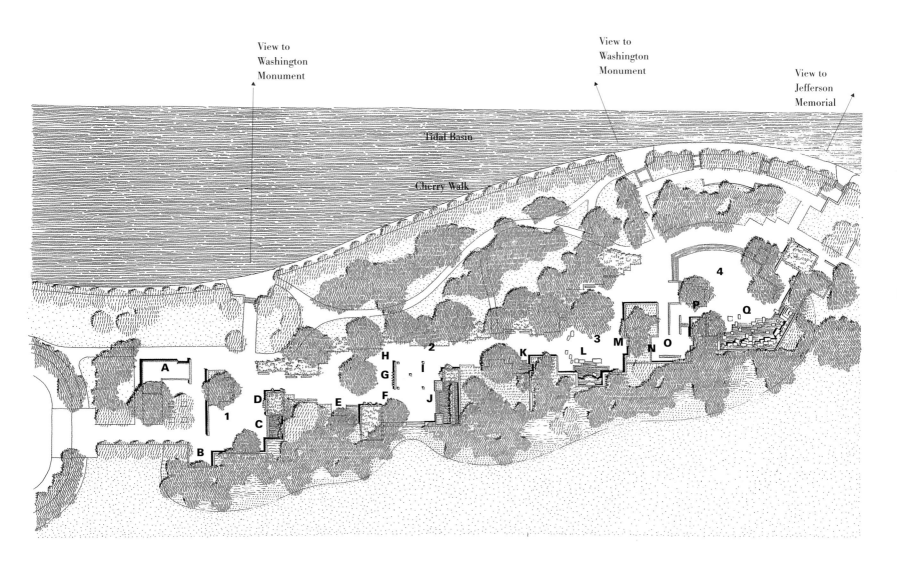

View to
Washington
Monument

View to
Washington
Monument

View to
Jefferson
Memorial

Tidal Basin

Cherry Walk

A

B

C

D

E

F

G

H

I

J

K

L

M

N

O

P

Q

1

2

3

4

0   100ft

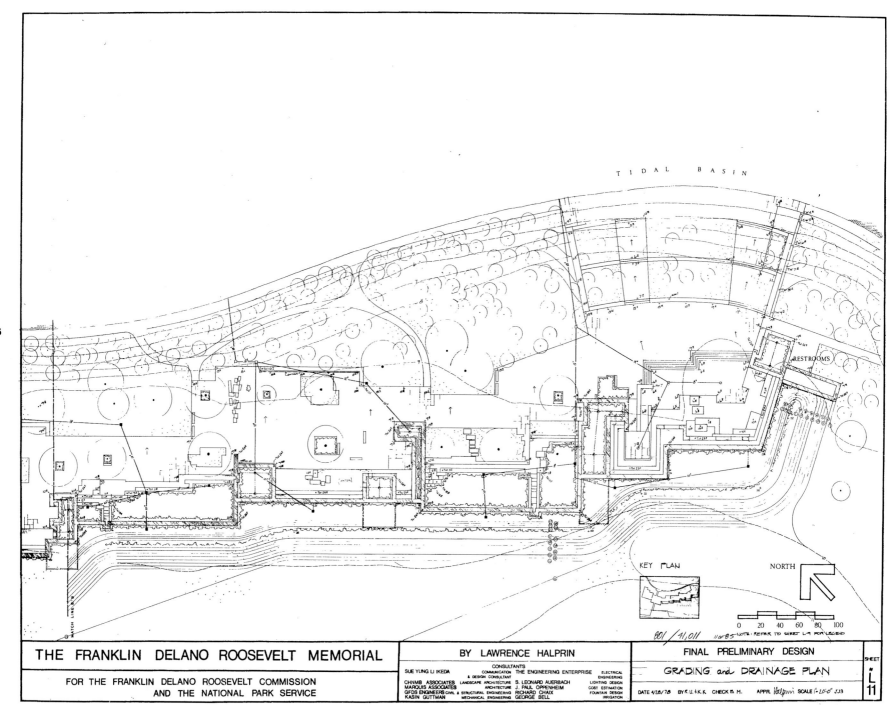

76

TIDAL BASIN

RESTROOMS

KEY PLAN

NORTH

0	20	40	60	80	100

THE FRANKLIN DELANO ROOSEVELT MEMORIAL

FOR THE FRANKLIN DELANO ROOSEVELT COMMISSION
AND THE NATIONAL PARK SERVICE

BY LAWRENCE HALPRIN

CONSULTANTS

SUE YUNG LI IKEDA — COMMUNICATION & DESIGN CONSULTANT — THE ENGINEERING ENTERPRISE — ELECTRICAL ENGINEERING
CHNMB ASSOCIATES — LANDSCAPE ARCHITECTURE — S. LEONARD AUERBACH — LIGHTING DESIGN
MARQUIS ASSOCIATES — ARCHITECTURE — J. PAUL OPPENHEIM — COST ESTIMATION
GFDS ENGINEERS CIVIL & STRUCTURAL ENGINEERING — RICHARD CHAIX — FOUNTAIN DESIGN
KASIN GUTTMAN — MECHANICAL ENGINEERING — GEORGE BELL — IRRIGATION

FINAL PRELIMINARY DESIGN

GRADING and DRAINAGE PLAN

DATE 4/28/78   BY R.U. & K.K.   CHECK B.M.   APPR. Halprin   SCALE 1"=20'-0"   JOB

SHEET
L
11

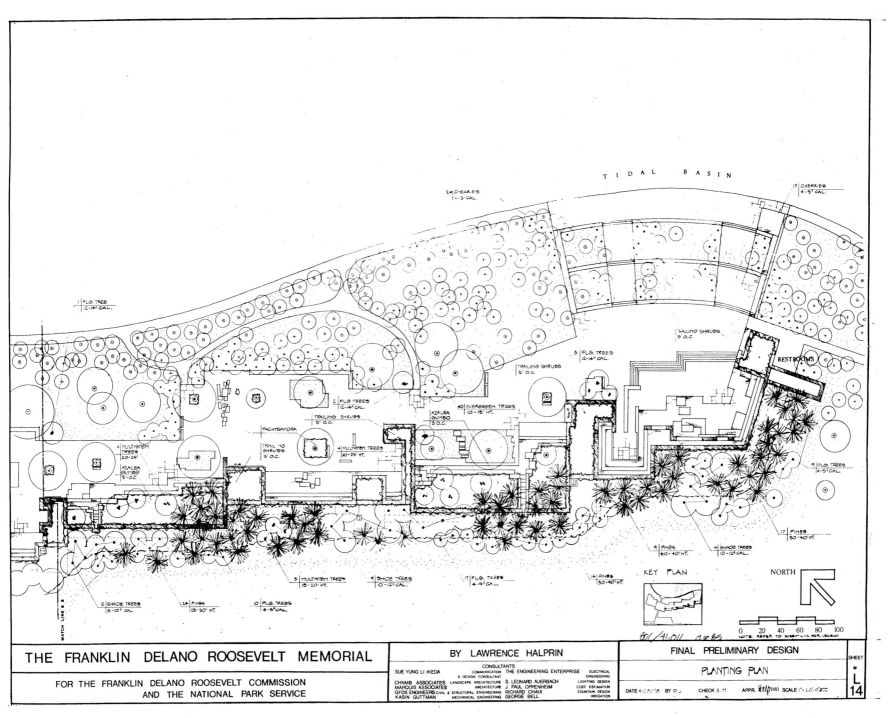

TIDAL BASIN

17 CHERRIES
4-5" CAL.

24 C-ERRIES
4-5" CAL.

1 FLG. TREE
12-14" CAL.

TRAILING SHRUBS
3' O.C.

RESTROOMS

3 FLG. TREES
12-14" CAL.

1 FLG. TREE
12-14" CAL.

TRAILING SHRUBS
3' O.C.

2 FLG. TREES
12-14" CAL.

40 EVERGREEN TREES
10-15' HT.

TRAILING SHRUBS
3' O.C.

PACHYSANDRA

AZALEA
GUMBO
3' O.C.

9 FLG. TREES
4-5" CAL.

4 MULTISTEM
TREES
20-25'

TRAILING
SHRUBS
3' O.C.

4 MULTISTEM TREES
20-25' HT.

AZALEA
GUMBO
3' O.C.

17 PINES
30-40' HT.

9 PINES
30-40' HT.

4 SHADE TREES
10-12" CAL.

3 MULTISTEM TREES
15-20' HT.

9 SHADE TREES
10-12" CAL.

17 FLG. TREES
4-5" CAL.

14 PINES
30-40' HT.

KEY PLAN

NORTH

5 SHADE TREES
8-10" CAL.

24 PINES
25-30' HT.

10 FLG. TREES
4-5" CAL.

MATCH LINE 8-8

0 20 40 60 80 100
NOTE: REFER TO SHEET L-12 FOR LEGEND

THE FRANKLIN DELANO ROOSEVELT MEMORIAL	BY LAWRENCE HALPRIN	FINAL PRELIMINARY DESIGN	SHEET

FOR THE FRANKLIN DELANO ROOSEVELT COMMISSION
AND THE NATIONAL PARK SERVICE

PLANTING PLAN

L
14

CONSULTANTS
SUE YUNG LI IKEDA COMMUNICATION THE ENGINEERING ENTERPRISE ELECTRICAL
& DESIGN CONSULTANT ENGINEERING
CHNMB ASSOCIATES LANDSCAPE ARCHITECTURE S. LEONARD AUERBACH LIGHTING DESIGN
MARQUIS ASSOCIATES ARCHITECTURE J. PAUL OPPENHEIM COST ESTIMATION
GFDS ENGINEERS CIVIL & STRUCTURAL ENGINEERING RICHARD CHAIX FOUNTAIN DESIGN
KASIN GUTTMAN MECHANICAL ENGINEERING GEORGE BELL IRRIGATION

DATE 4/25/78 BY D.J. CHECK B.M. APPR. Halprin SCALE 1"=20'-0"

Planting Plan

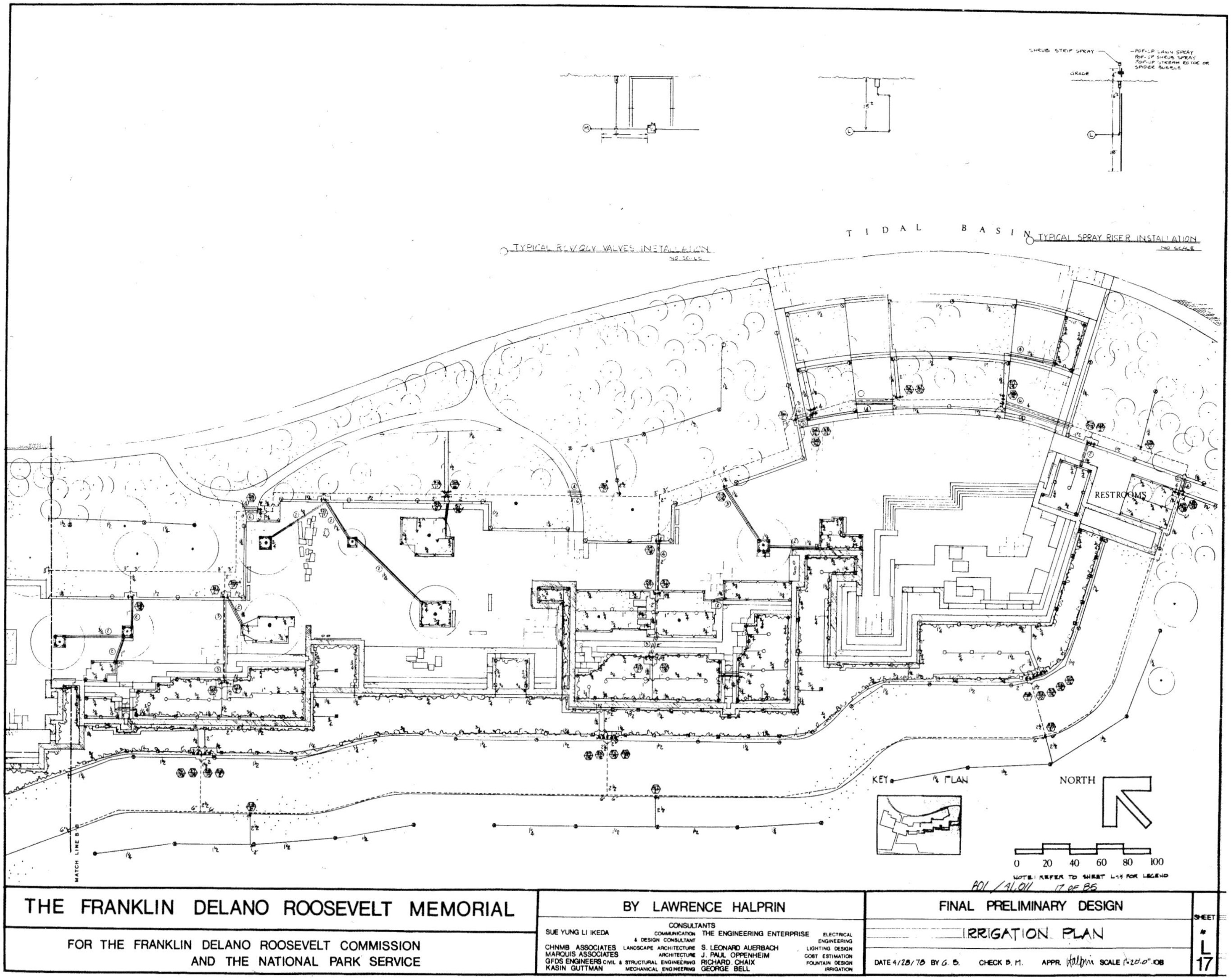

TIDAL BASIN

TYPICAL R.V/C.V VALVES INSTALLATION

TYPICAL SPRAY RISER INSTALLATION
NO SCALE

RESTROOMS

KEY PLAN

NORTH

0 20 40 60 80 100

NOTE: REFER TO SHEET L-19 FOR LEGEND

THE FRANKLIN DELANO ROOSEVELT MEMORIAL	BY LAWRENCE HALPRIN	FINAL PRELIMINARY DESIGN	SHEET
FOR THE FRANKLIN DELANO ROOSEVELT COMMISSION AND THE NATIONAL PARK SERVICE	CONSULTANTS	IRRIGATION PLAN	L 17

SUE YUNG LI IKEDA — COMMUNICATION — THE ENGINEERING ENTERPRISE — ELECTRICAL ENGINEERING
& DESIGN CONSULTANT
CHNMB ASSOCIATES — LANDSCAPE ARCHITECTURE — S. LEONARD AUERBACH — LIGHTING DESIGN
MARQUIS ASSOCIATES — ARCHITECTURE — J. PAUL OPPENHEIM — COST ESTIMATION
GFDS ENGINEERS — CIVIL & STRUCTURAL ENGINEERING — RICHARD CHAIX — FOUNTAIN DESIGN
KASIN GUTTMAN — MECHANICAL ENGINEERING — GEORGE BELL — IRRIGATION

DATE 4/28/78 BY G. B.   CHECK B. M.   APPR. Halprin SCALE 1"-20'-0".IOB

Irrigation Plan

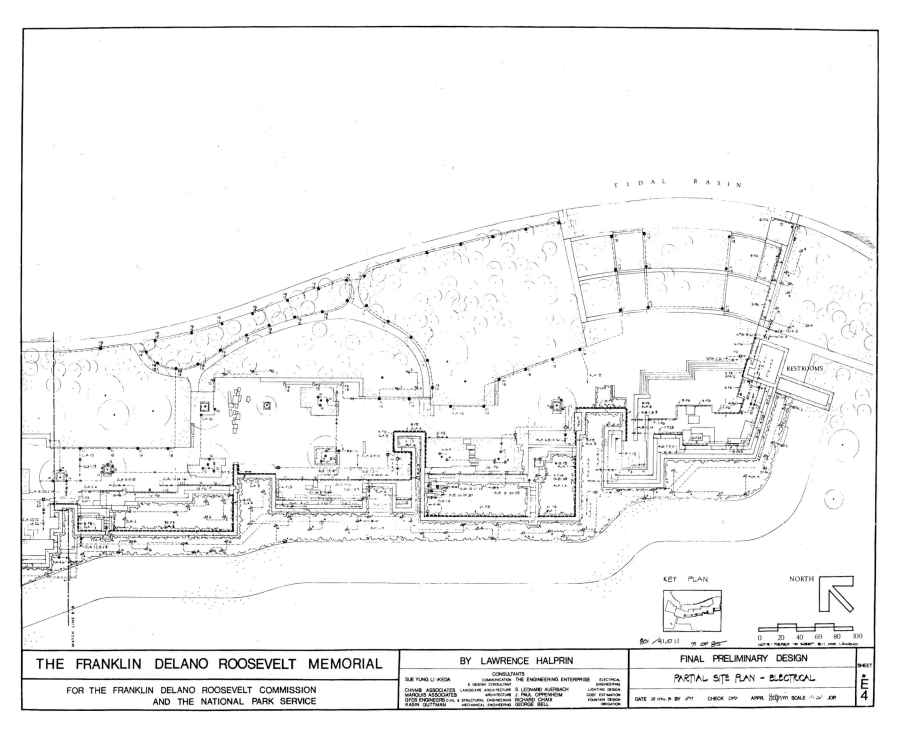

TIDAL BASIN

RESTROOMS

KEY PLAN

NORTH

0 20 40 60 80 100

THE FRANKLIN DELANO ROOSEVELT MEMORIAL	BY LAWRENCE HALPRIN	FINAL PRELIMINARY DESIGN	SHEET
FOR THE FRANKLIN DELANO ROOSEVELT COMMISSION AND THE NATIONAL PARK SERVICE	CONSULTANTS	PARTIAL SITE PLAN - ELECTRICAL	E 4

SUE YUNG LI IKEDA — COMMUNICATION & DESIGN CONSULTANT — THE ENGINEERING ENTERPRISE — ELECTRICAL ENGINEERING
CHNMB ASSOCIATES — LANDSCAPE ARCHITECTURE — S. LEONARD AUERBACH — LIGHTING DESIGN
MARQUIS ASSOCIATES — ARCHITECTURE — J. PAUL OPPENHEIM — COST ESTIMATION
GFDS ENGINEERS — CIVIL & STRUCTURAL ENGINEERING — RICHARD CHAIX — FOUNTAIN DESIGN
KASIN GUTTMAN — MECHANICAL ENGINEERING — GEORGE BELL — IRRIGATION

DATE 28 APRIL 78 BY JFH   CHECK DFD   APPR. Halprin SCALE 1"=20' JOP.

Electrical Plan

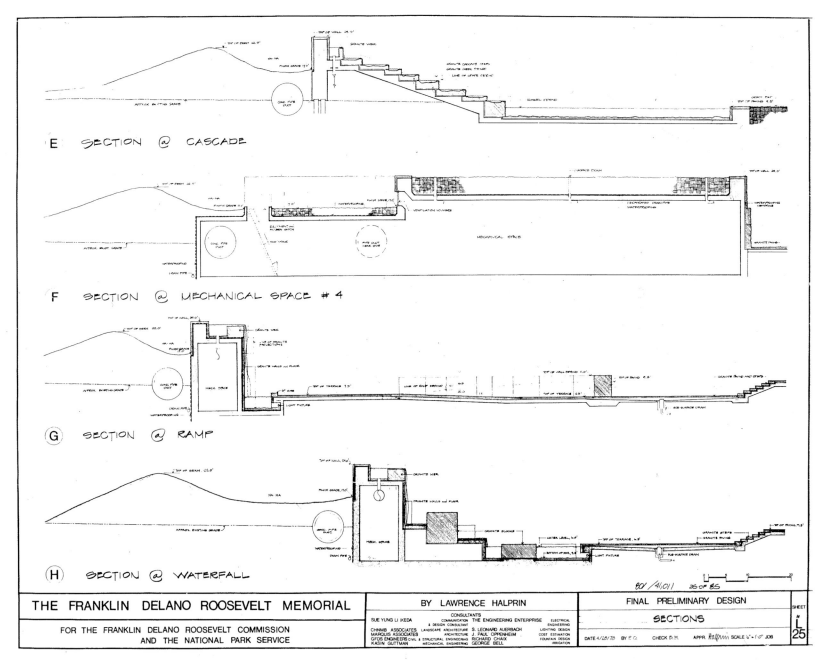

E SECTION @ CASCADE

F SECTION @ MECHANICAL SPACE # 4

G SECTION @ RAMP

H SECTION @ WATERFALL

THE FRANKLIN DELANO ROOSEVELT MEMORIAL	BY LAWRENCE HALPRIN	FINAL PRELIMINARY DESIGN	SHEET
FOR THE FRANKLIN DELANO ROOSEVELT COMMISSION AND THE NATIONAL PARK SERVICE	CONSULTANTS	SECTIONS	L 25

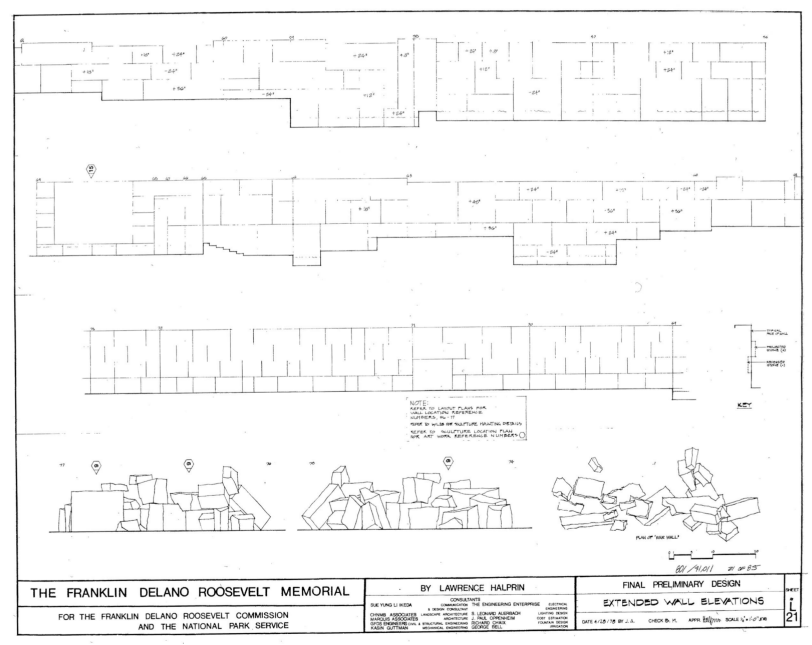

NOTE:
REFER TO LAYOUT PLANS FOR
WALL LOCATION REFERENCE
NUMBERS, PL - 77

REFER TO WLIB FOR SCULPTURE MOUNTING DETAILS

REFER TO SCULPTURE LOCATION PLAN
FOR ART WORK REFERENCE NUMBERS

KEY

PLAN OF "WAR WALL"

801 /91,011   21 OF 85

THE FRANKLIN DELANO ROOSEVELT MEMORIAL	BY LAWRENCE HALPRIN	FINAL PRELIMINARY DESIGN	SHEET
FOR THE FRANKLIN DELANO ROOSEVELT COMMISSION AND THE NATIONAL PARK SERVICE	CONSULTANTS	EXTENDED WALL ELEVATIONS	L 21

Sections

April 1945	Franklin Delano Roosevelt dies in Warm Springs, Georgia.
August 1955	Franklin Delano Roosevelt Memorial Commission established.
June 1958	West Potomac Park chosen for memorial.
January–September 1960	First design competition garners 574 entries.
December 1960	William Pedersen and Bradford Tilney of New York City named winners of the competition.
January 1962	FDR Memorial Commission approves revised Pedersen and Tilney design.
June 1962	Commission of Fine Arts rejects design.
June 1964	Commission of Fine Arts approves revised Pedersen and Tilney design.
April 1965	Faced with unyielding opposition from the public and the Roosevelt family, Pedersen and Tilney resign.
January 1966	Marcel Breuer chosen to design memorial.
January 1967	Breuer design rejected by Commission of Fine Arts.
January 1969	Breuer resigns.
May 1974	Landscape architect Lawrence Halprin chosen to design memorial.
March 1978	FDR Memorial Commission and Commission of Fine Arts approve Halprin's design.
March 1981	House authorizes construction of memorial.
July 1981	Senate authorizes construction.
September 1991	Groundbreaking ceremony.
October 1994	Memorial construction begins.
May 1997	Memorial opens to the public.

Notes

1 Justice Felix Frankfurter, "What FDR Wanted," *Atlantic Monthly*, March 1961, 39-40.

2 All Halprin quotations are from interviews conducted by the author between May and October 1997.

3 Gerald W. Johnson, "Memorial to FDR," *New Republic*, September 21, 1959, 16.

4 Taken from Chairman Biddle's December 30, 1960, press conference on the winning design.

5 Other jury members were landscape architect Thomas Church; Bartlett Hayes Jr., director of the Addison Gallery of American Art, Phillips Andover Academy; Joseph Hudnut, professor of architecture, Harvard University; and Paul Rudolph, chairman of the Department of Architecture at Yale University.

6 Letter to the *New York Times*, January 10, 1961. For a revealing survey of professional and critical reaction, see *Architectural Forum*, April 1961, 187-88.

7 Testimony before the House Administration Subcommittee, June 8, 1962.

8 Quoted in *Time*, January 13, 1961, 60.

9 Henry Hope Reed, letter to the *New York Times*, February 12, 1961.

10 Remarks from the minutes of the Commision of Fine Arts meeting, January 25, 1967.

11 The other architects and landscape architects interviewed by the Commission were Edward Durrell Stone Jr., John Carl Warnecke, Eric Gugler, Hideo Sasaki, William Johnson and Robert Zion.

12 *Washington Post*, August 8, 1981, B7.

13 An informative summary of these sessions appeared in Malcolm Carter's, "The FDR Memorial: A Monument to Politics, Bureaucracy and the Art of Accommodation," *Art News*, October 1978, 50-57.

Photography and Drawings

Alan Ward
Photographs: Cover, pages 21, 39, 41, 43-73, 84

Franklin Delano Roosevelt Library
Photographs: Pages 5-19. Page 6 INP (left), UPI (right). Page 7 OWI (top). Page 9 James A. Farley (bottom). Page 10 UPI Acme (left). Page 11 USSP (bottom). Page 12 UPI Acme (left). Page 13 Wide World (left). Page 15, 16, 17 Margaret Suckley.

National Archives
Photographs and drawings: Pages 23-26, 28-29, 31.

National Park Service
Drawings: Pages 35, 76-81. Photographs: Pages 80-81 Jane Hanna.

Office of Lawrence Halprin
Photographs: Page 37 Paul Scardina.

Peter Walker and Partners
Photographs: Pages 33-34.

"I believe that we have been right in the course we have charted. To abandon our purpose of building a greater, a more stable, and a more tolerant America would be to miss the tide and perhaps to miss the port. I propose to sail ahead. I feel sure that your hopes and I feel sure that your help are with me. For to reach a port, we must sail—sail, not lie at anchor, sail, not drift." —Franklin Delano Roosevelt, Fireside Chat, April 14, 1938.